MW01528774

ow Do Volcanoes Explode?

Showing Events and Processes

Seth Matthas

COMPUTER KIDS
Powered by Computational Thinking

PowerKiDS
press.

Published in 2018 by The Rosen Publishing Group, Inc.
29 East 21st Street, New York, NY 10010

Book Design: Jennifer Ryder-Talbot
Editor: Caitie McAneney

Photo Credits: Cover Ammit Jack/Shutterstock.com; p. 5 Bos11/
Shutterstock.com; p. 6-7 Byelikova Oksana/Shutterstock.com; p. 8-9 Designua/
Shutterstock.com; p. 10-11 Ami Parikh/Shutterstock.com; p. 12, 15, 16 Santhosh
Varghese/Shutterstock.com; p. 18-19 Fredy Thuerig/Shutterstock.com; p. 20 Linnas/
Shutterstock.com.

Library of Congress Cataloging-in-Publication Data

Names: Matthas, Seth.
Title: How do volcanoes explode?: showing events and processes / Seth Matthas.
Description: New York : Rosen Classroom, 2018. | Series: Computer Kids: Powered by
Computational Thinking | Includes glossary and index.
Identifiers: LCCN ISBN 9781508137900 (pbk.) | ISBN 9781538324028 (library bound) |
ISBN 9781538355275 (6pack) | ISBN 9781538352892 (ebook)
Subjects: LCSH: Volcanoes--Juvenile literature. | Volcanoes--Experiments--Juvenile
literature. | Science projects--Juvenile literature.
Classification: LCC QE521.3 M38 2018 | DDC 551.21--dc23

Manufactured in the United States of America

CPSIA Compliance Information: Batch #WS18RC: For Further Information contact Rosen Publishing, New York, New York at 1-800-237-9932

Table of Contents

Volcanoes

Have you ever seen a volcano? Volcanoes are some of the scariest **landforms** on Earth. They are openings in Earth's surface through which lava and gas can get out. This lava, which is **molten** rock, comes from a very hot layer of Earth underground. When it's underground, lava is called magma.

Some volcanoes are inactive, or don't pose much of a risk. Other volcanoes are very active, **erupting** often. They can cause a great deal of **destruction** to people who live nearby.

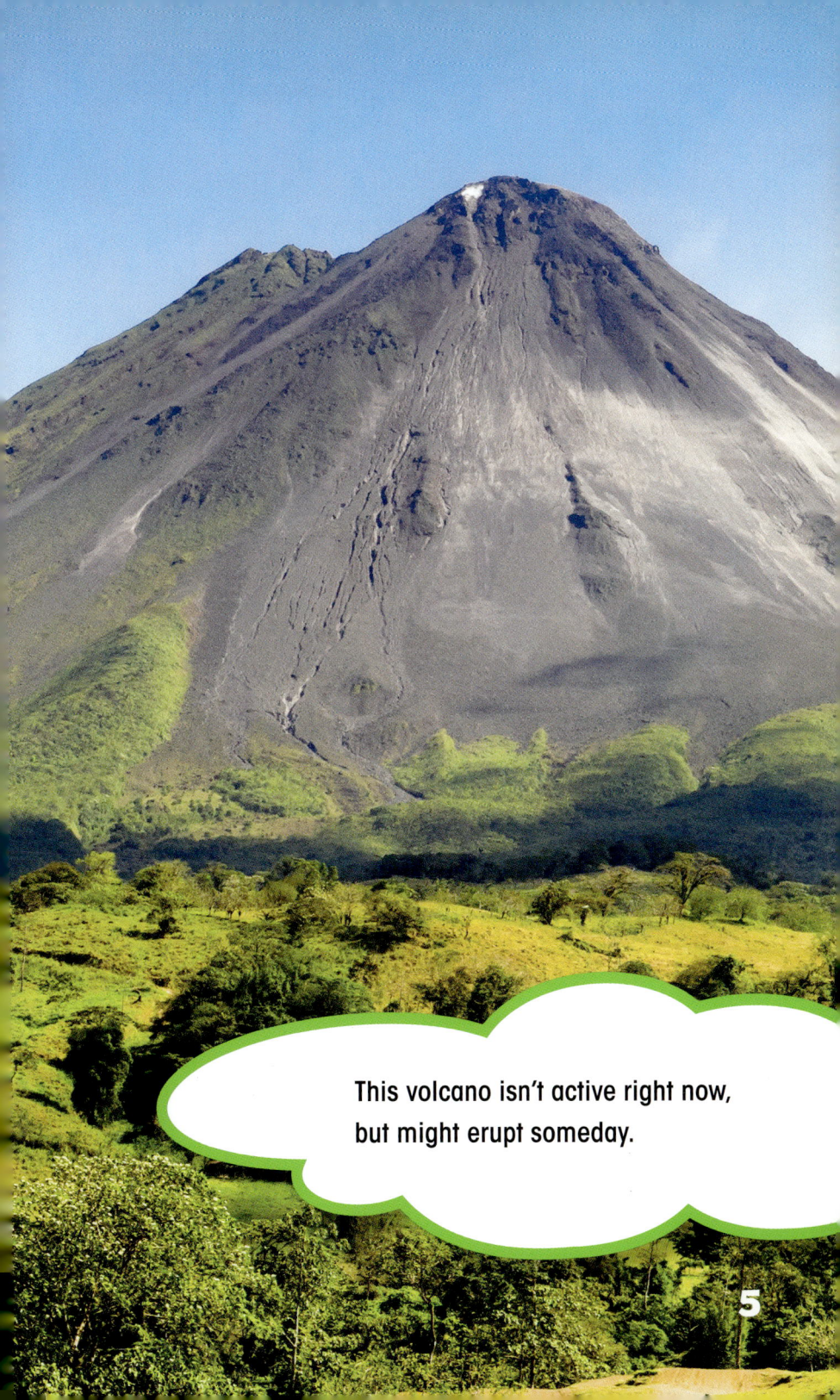

This volcano isn't active right now, but might erupt someday.

Volcanic eruptions can create huge gray clouds of ash and debris that travel many miles away.

Volcanic Eruptions

About 1,500 volcanoes might be active around the world. That means they may let out gas, debris, or lava.

Volcanic eruptions are a way of Earth letting off pressure. Imagine shaking a bottle of soda. Gas bubbles are locked inside, creating pressure. When you open the bottle, the pressure is released and the soda erupts. Lava has the ability to burn everything in its way. It might cool and turn into harmful boulders. Some volcanoes let out poisonous ash and gas.

Simulating Tectonic Plates

Why do volcanoes happen? Volcanoes usually exist along plate **boundaries**. That's where two tectonic plates meet. Earth is like a puzzle. Tectonic plates are the slabs of hard earth that come together to complete the puzzle. The tectonic plates move because they're sitting on a hot, plastic-like layer.

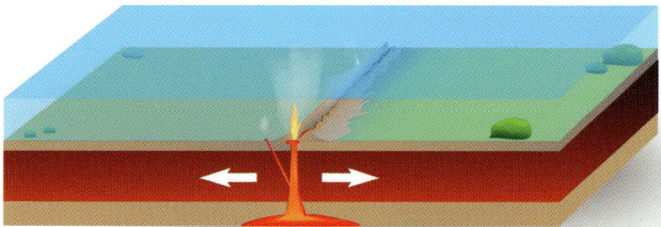

divergent boundary

These illustrations show how volcanoes can form along convergent and divergent boundaries.

Tectonic plates come together at convergent boundaries. They pull apart at divergent boundaries. They slide past one another at transform boundaries. Volcanoes may form at convergent or divergent boundaries. Tectonic plate **simulations** show how this movement causes trenches, mountains, and volcanoes to form.

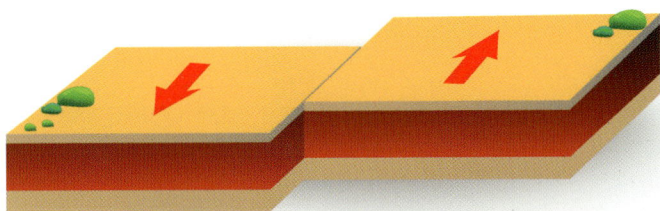

transform boundary

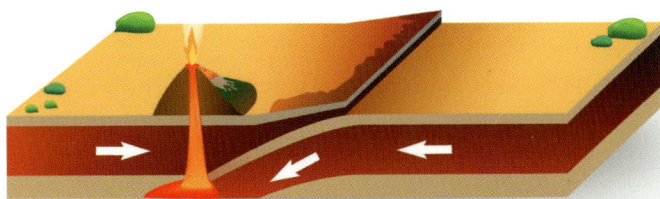

convergent boundary

Different Kinds
of Volcanoes

Most active volcanoes are in the Pacific Ring of Fire. That's an area around the edges of the Pacific Ocean.

This is a cinder cone volcano with a large crater.

If you don't live in an area with volcanoes, you may never see one up close. That's why models and photographs of volcanoes are important. By looking at models, or likenesses, you can see that volcanoes are different shapes and sizes. Cinder cone volcanoes have a single vent and wide **crater**. Composite volcanoes are larger with smaller craters. Shield volcanoes have gentle slopes with wide bases.

You can paint your model to look like a real volcano.

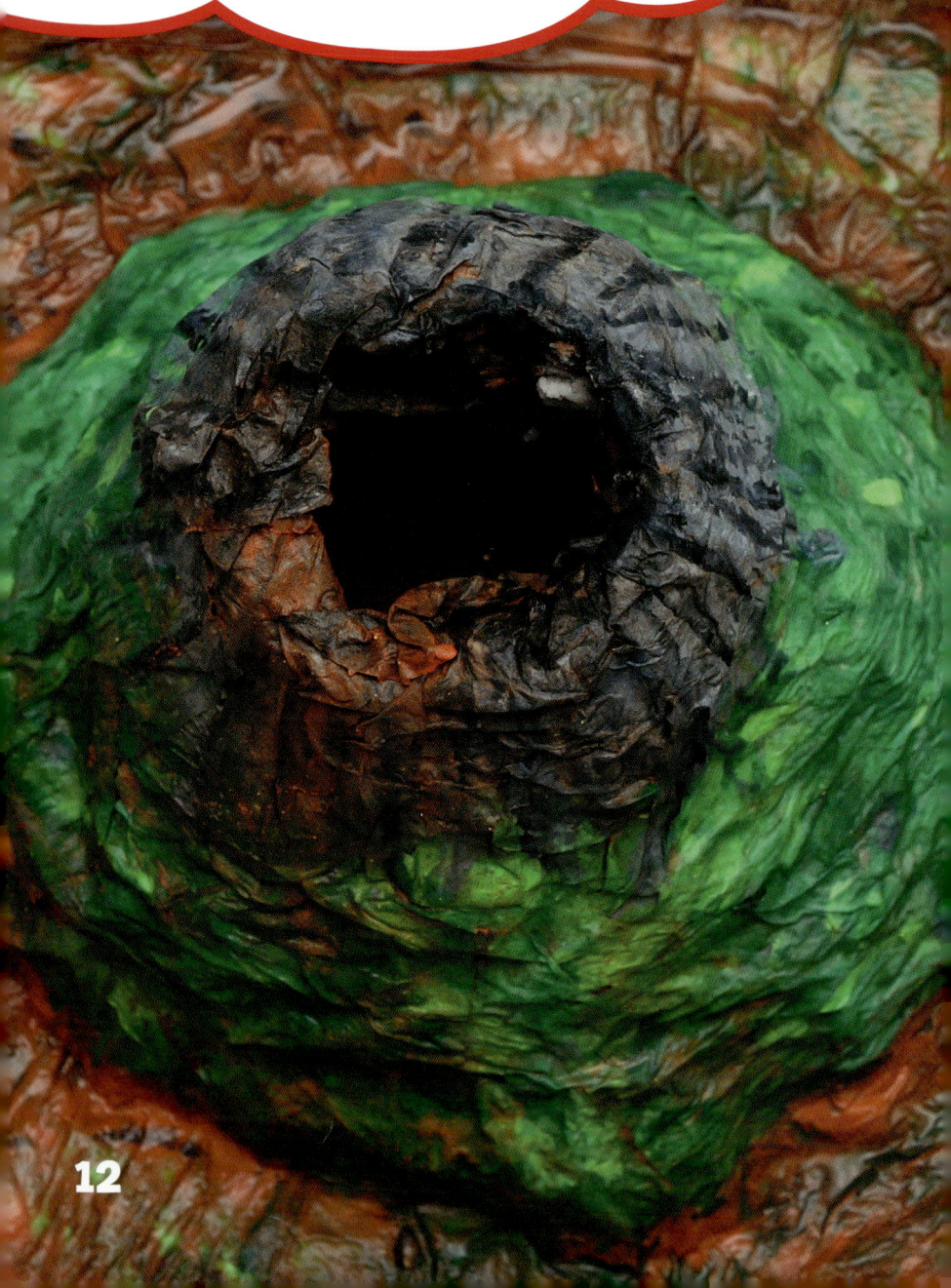

Build Your Volcano

You can make a model of a volcano at home. People build volcano models using different kinds of **materials**. Some people take an empty soda bottle and cover it with brown clay to look like a volcano.

You can also make a **paper-mache** volcano. To do this, dip strips of newspaper into a mixture of white glue and water. Then, cover a soda bottle with the material, leaving the mouth of the bottle open. Keep adding paper-mache to make the correct volcano shape.

A Chemical Reaction

You can add toy animals, cars, buildings, and trees to your model. They could represent, or stand for, the things that might be destroyed by an eruption.

Next, you have to mix chemicals together to simulate an eruption. Use a tool called a funnel to pour three tablespoons of baking soda into the bottle mouth. Then, put a few drops of red food dye in. That will make the lava look red. The ingredient that will cause a **chemical reaction** is white vinegar. That's the last thing to add.

The two main ingredients for this chemical reaction are baking soda and white vinegar.

What can you learn from the eruption simulation?

Eruption

When the vinegar hits the baking soda, the chemical reaction will occur. The mixture will produce a gas and a liquid. It will erupt through the mouth of the bottle. The "lava" will flow down the sides of the volcano, perhaps causing destruction to the toys you placed there.

This simulates the eruption of a volcano. Like a volcanic eruption, pressure built up inside the vent until it had to be let out. The lava likely shot out of the bottle, causing a mess. Likewise, a volcanic eruption is destructive and messy.

Destruction

Some scientists believe that more than 260,000 people have died as a result of volcanic eruptions in the past 300 years. Lava can sweep people, animals, and houses away. Boulders and mudslides can bury and crush all in their path. Ash and gas may be harmful when people breathe them in.

You can see the amount of destruction that might occur if you put toys in the path of your volcano model. They might be swept away by the force of the lava. Now imagine if your lava was very hot!

This house was destroyed by a real-life volcanic eruption!

Some scientists go right into an active volcano's path to collect data and samples.

Predicting Eruptions

Can scientists predict when a volcano might erupt? Volcanologists, or people who study volcanoes, have tools and methods for predicting an eruption.

Scientists can look at a volcano's past eruptions to see what they were like. They may put **sensors** at different places on the volcano. The sensors can collect data on volcanic gases and underground magma movement. Scientists use this data to make a prediction that an eruption may occur. This helps them warn people so they can **evacuate** the area.

How Are Simulations Used?

Simulations and models are often used to teach people about natural disasters, such as volcanic eruptions. Models can show you what volcanoes look like. Simulations can show how tectonic plates move and how a volcanic eruption might affect those around it.

Scientists also use simulations of weather systems to predict massive storms before they happen. Using data and information from past storms and disasters, scientists can create a simulation of a storm's path. Simulations help us safely see natural disasters up close!

Glossary

boundary: A dividing line.

chemical reaction: A chemical change that occurs when two or more substances combine.

crater: A bowl-shaped hole on the surface of a planet or moon.

destruction: The state of being destroyed or ruined.

erupt: To burst forth.

evacuate: To withdraw from a place for protection.

landform: A natural feature of a land surface.

material: Something from which something else can be made.

molten: Changed into a liquid form by heat.

paper-mache: A light, strong molding material of wastepaper and glue.

sensor: A tool that can detect changes in its surroundings.

simulation: An object or event that shows or acts like another object or event.

Index